The Key

UNLOCKING PROFITS
EXISTING IN YOUR BUSINESS

Ben Sillem

ISBN 978-1-9991075-0-5

First Printing, 2019

Printed in Canada

Table of Contents

Disclaimer

This is a work of fiction. Names, characters, business, events, and incidents are the product of the author's imagination. However, Canadian winters are very real and very cold. Any resemblance to actual persons, living or dead, or actual events is purely coincidental. Space and time have been rearranged to suit the convenience of the book. The author is not an insurance broker and makes no claim to the accuracy of the insurance topics discussed herein.

Commute

IT HAD ALREADY BEEN a busy morning. Robert had been volun-told to get the children to school on his way to work this morning. Who was he to say no to Queen Bee? Especially, after the two of them had enjoyed a nice weekend celebrating their 15th wedding anniversary. They still enjoyed each other's company and had two semi-normal kids to show for it. A son and a daughter, eleven and thirteen, respectively.

Slithering along the slippery, snowy, Southern Alberta winter roads was never anyone's idea of a good time. Robert, nonetheless, trusted the all wheel drive SUV he enjoyed driving. The Audi Sportswagon was a steady steed in all difficult conditions. More so with the Blizzak winter tires he had purchased last fall. He patted himself on the back for having the foresight to be concerned about winter driving some months ago. He relaxed a little and smiled as he watched others in vehicles not so well equipped suffer their way through the conditions. He couldn't sip on the champagne of schadenfreude for too long as he had things to do. With one eye on the road and the other on the clock, his thoughts drifted to his to-do list.

A blast from the past sounded through the car speakers showcasing the Bangles singing Just Another Manic Monday. Robert cursed saying no to the dealer when offered the Sirius XM Satellite radio package when he bought the vehicle a couple of years ago. Local radio was getting worse by the day. Could you play a more obvious song, Robert thought, aren't they all, his negative thoughts cascading without any conscious effort on his part. OK, get it together, he chastised himself. What's on tap this morning? Kids to school for 08:30. Unlikely, as it is now 08:30 and he has at least ten minutes still of drive time. Longer if he has to stare at the bumper of this mutton head in the Mazda much longer. Get a grip, literally and figuratively. The only thing missing from this guy's bumper was a sticker evidencing he was an Oilers fan. Had to be. I can't believe the Flames lost last night. Robert's mind was all over the place. OK, where was I? Things could align and I might, maybe, possibly get to the office just a few minutes late for our weekly touch-point meeting scheduled for 09:00. From here, Robert's day remained full. He had a separate meeting with his VP Technology, a lunch with a member of his management team, and then a meeting with one of their vendors to cap off the day's schedule. Running an insurance brokerage wasn't just about shaking hands and selling insurance anymore.

Glancing at the car clock Robert was disheartened to see it was now 08:50 as he pulled into J. Kenney Junior

High School parking lot. He was further miffed with himself to realize that he had been so consumed by the chatter inside his mind that he hadn't spent any of the drive talking with his children. He wished them a good day and sent them on their way. They were just as happy to get out of the car and drifted into the crowd of other sleepy eyed children who all appeared as unprepared for the winter weather.

Off Robert went burning rubber in the direction of his office. Wishful thinking, burning rubber, it was -25C and nothing was being burned but gasoline. Traffic continued to conspire to keep Robert creeping to his destination. March can't come soon enough he thought. Their annual family Spring holiday was set for an all inclusive resort on the Mexican Riviera. How nice the warm sand and cold drinks will feel. It seemed like a lifetime in the distance relative to the cold, still dark he found himself in presently.

Somehow, the roads slowly cleared themselves of traffic and Robert made a bit of progress. He arrived at the office at 09:15. Although it was just the start of the day, he felt stressed, agitated, and like he had been through an emotional washing machine for hours already. He further chastised himself, come on Bob, get it together, you own this place, you need to set the standard for what's professional and how we all want to behave. Sure you're late, but it's how you handle yourself now that matters more.

As Robert gathered himself and entered the boardroom where their Monday morning Touchpoint meeting was well underway, he was grateful to see that Janet hadn't missed a beat. She had taken charge of the meeting and things seemed to be progressing well. All other members of the team had managed to assemble themselves on time. He received a few welcome good morning nods while Janet continued leading the meeting. Janet was Bob's right hand. Her official title was Chief Operating Officer. She had steadfastly been with Bob's brokerage since before Bob even worked there. Janet knew more about the insurance business than Flo from Progressive.

The balance of the Management Group, Tom from Finance, Jason from IT, and Sue from Sales took up the remaining seats at the table. Janet was just wrapping up a summation of this week's plans. As Janet wound down, Robert apologized for being late. Tom not being able to help himself offered, "I've heard a joke the other day on the radio, "A guy shows up late for work, his boss exclaims incredulously, "Where were you!, You should have been here at 08:30!" The man asks inquisitively, "Why, what happened at 08:30?"

The others at the table smiled nervously at Tom's attempt at humor. Robert said, "Good morning everyone. Thanks for the 'joke', Tom. I apologize for being late. The drive in was a bear. I am impressed to see everyone else made it in without issues. I'm even more impressed to see that Janet has taken care of things and gotten our week off to a good start. I hope the rest of our day today goes as smoothly."

Technology Travails

IT WAS ANOTHER AREA of Robert's business that seemed to be avalanching up hill from a small, fringe thought, to an all encompassing, ever growing concern that became the mountain overshadowing any other business conversation A Priori seemed to be having. He was slowly coming to the realization that his knowledge of IT was enough to be dangerous and not enough to be useful. The expertise implied was significant and ever shifting. The conversation was constant and swung from committing to a full in house IT program all the way to trying to outsource every aspect of IT to specialists. Both approaches had their strengths and weaknesses. A Priori had been managed in recent years with a bit of a hybrid approach where Jason did what he could internally and the business leaned heavily on outside resources in other areas. Locked in step with the constancy of IT conversations was an intertwined constancy of cost creep.

Robert met with Jason in Jason's office. Like most IT guys, Jason was tucked into a dark office on the 3rd floor stuffed floor to ceiling with an arsenal of computer parts that Robert couldn't make heads or tails of. He was hoping that Jason knew what Robert didn't. They commiserated over the morning's commute even though Jason seemed to struggle less getting in than had Robert. Jason then got right to the point. "Bob, I know you were hoping we'd be able to postpone talk related to upgrading our email servers, but we're pushing capacity here. We're running at 80% and our email volumes are mushrooming. That's IT speak for growing exponentially. Which is IT speak for growing a lot." A lot is something Robert definitely understood. What he didn't understand was the "humor" that IT folk always seemed to attempt. Robert asked, "Jason, what are our options here? Should we abandon these servers and move off site? Or something else?"

Robert regretted asking the question as soon as he heard the words leaving his mouth. Jason had a special gift of making a short story long and relished the opportunity of elucidating his expertise eloquently. "Presently, A Priori has set up and is maintaining our own email servers. This is a complicated and time consuming process that is monopolizing both my time and skill set. Our email server utilizes numerous components. I need to be well versed in our Mail Transfer Agent, Mail Delivery Agent, and both IMAP and POP3 protocols." Jason continued, "You may well know that the MTA, Mail Transfer Agent handles the simple message transfer protocol traffic or SMTP." Of course, Robert didn't know and he knew full well that Jason knew he didn't know, but they both continued to pretend each understood what was being talked about.

Robert began to wish he was back in his Sportwagon behind the bumper of the Mazda. The tenseness of burgeoning road rage was total tranquility relative to the brain drain being incurred. Robert, interjected, "Jason, I appreciate you're busy and have many irons in the fire, can you run with this initiative and seek to provide a recommended course of action by the end of the month? Perhaps, you would be kind enough to include assessments as to urgency – how long do we have before our current arrangement becomes unreliable, and what does unreliable mean? That is, what risks do we face and when associated with our current email hosting arrangement? Additionally, detailing project cost and timeline associated with recommendation would also be appreciated." Jason recognizing Robert's urgency, nodded his head, made some notes, and agreed to offer some option for discussion within the next two weeks.

Jason then asked, "Bob, do you have time to chat about Sue's project?" Sue was A Priori's VP Sales. She was aggressively advocating for a technology upgrade to be used to generate online leads. Robert wasn't a complete dinosaur, he could see where the world was heading. He knew that Insurance sales were likely to be done increasingly online, at least in some capacity, for some coverages. He knew he had no option but to do something in this area, he just didn't know where to begin or what was important to consider. Robert lost in his own thoughts must have offered some kind of acknowledgement to Jason as he continued talking, "Sue has some great ideas. She's done some serious legwork and sourced several options for Online Lead Generation. It seems she definitely has a preference. My concern, though, is that she hasn't involved either me or others on the Management Team in her search to date." Jason stopped talking and looked at Robert, hoping that Robert would understand what Jason was trying to say without him having to say it. Robert deployed the oldest leadership trick in the book and displayed a stoic face saying nothing. Jason couldn't help himself and continued talking, "Any selection of software should certainly include IT in the evaluation process. We need to know what we're getting ourselves into. Some of the options are inevitably going to have far reaching implications beyond just sales. Bob, I need your help to encourage Sue to bring the balance of the Management Team into the conversation sooner than later." Robert appreciated Jason's openness and let him know that he would draft a memo to the Team seeking to make this an agenda item for next week's Monday Touchpoint meeting.

"Bob, we'll also need to make time to discuss Phones." We have a service contract expiring and our current vendor is chomping to commit A Priori to a three year extension. Technology is advancing steadily on this front as well. We should consider our options here and look at alternate vendors with expanded capabilities. For example, we could seek some automated reception services as well as digital call recording. These do come at additional costs but offer the business prospective benefits...." Robert cut Jason off, before Jason could continue expounding upon his view of benefits for new phones. Robert said, "I don't have bandwidth for this conversation now. I need some time to prepare for another meeting coming up shortly. Let's diarize this to discuss one on one in a couple of weeks."

Robert's mind was reeling from the short conversation with Jason. The three projects briefly discussed all seemed pressing issues. How was he supposed to determine how to prioritize amongst these when he didn't even understand the implications associated with each? IT expense was an ever growing item on the Income Statement. It was also becoming the second biggest allocation of Capital Expenditures outside of book acquisitions. Was he running an Insurance Brokerage or a Software firm? Sometimes it was tough to know. No matter what resources A Priori allocated to this area, there was always another must have technology project waiting in the wings. Robert wondered if other brokerages felt the same way. Sometimes it seemed like not making a decision was a good one as whatever is the new, flashy, latest and greatest, whiz bang software becomes obsolete within a year or two. One is rewarded for waiting for the next great thing. Robert reminisced about when he started at A Priori as a CSR working for his father's firm. Life was much simpler then. All he had to do was learn a little about some insurance words and hang out with people. That was a life he missed. When was the last time he had called on a customer? Who was the last customer he had even had a conversation with? As his thoughts thrashed, he was jarred back to the present by the ringing of his phone.

Hiccup

PICKING UP THE RECEIVER, Robert saw it was a call from one of his Commercial producers. "Good morning Josh", Robert said into the phone. Josh responded in a somewhat subdued tone. He said, "Bob, I'll get right to the point, I've got some bad news." Robert listened as Josh recounted the reasons for his call. Josh has been with A Priori Insurance for just over a year and had been a solid performer. He had been in the top three in terms of new business development for the last three quarters. As a reward for his success, and as a result of Josh asking Robert, Josh had been rewarded by getting some additional accounts assigned to him. It appears that during the transition of moving some accounts to Josh some coverage for a client in the transportation business had been overlooked. The client had an accident, was seeking to make a claim, and the gap in coverage was now revealed.

The client was a trucking company that had a fleet of flatbed trailers it used to transport equipment to construction sites. Its business activities were seasonal and during lulls in the action, they would seek to minimize coverage on inactive trailers in order to reduce insurance expense. It seems that they had begun a busier time. In the process they had sent over information to A Priori indicating that they needed trailers x and y to get additional insurance in place as they would be in action imminently. This paperwork was missed by A Priori, presumably, by Josh. We didn't inform the insurance company and formally put coverage in place. An employee of the client had an accident driving one of these trailers and damage resulted. They contacted who they understood their insurance company to be in order to initiate a claim only to be informed that they did not have coverage in place. Needless to say the client is more than a little bit upset and that disappointment is falling at A Priori's feet in the form of anger.

Robert sighed deeply while listening to Josh recount the client's frustrations. Josh was also injecting his own irritation. He noted, "why do insureds think they can just send over something in an email or even in a text and think that we've both received and acted on it immediately. They need to be responsible for making sure they have formal verification that something is insured before they assume it is. I don't understand how this is our problem, Bob. I think we can push back here." Robert considered the information provided so far. The client had been an A Priori customer for ten plus years. They paid their bills on time and purchased well over $30,000 a year in premiums. Their business was a steady and proven one. It wasn't going anywhere. This client had a solid history of success and if A Priori played its cards correctly, the relationship had the chance to be salvaged and remain a customer for the foreseeable future. It would make no sense to be indignant with them. Robert with hopes of getting Josh's thoughts on a more useful subject asked, "Do we know the extent of the claim? Was anyone hurt? Is it just physical damage? What numbers are we talking about for repairs? Have you completed our loss report form, Josh, and submitted to Janet?" Josh admitted that he didn't yet have answers to most of these questions. He'd just been on the receiving end of getting an earful from a scared and stressed customer. "The customer doesn't know the exact damage yet, he figured it was in the neighborhood of $15,000, but had the trailer picked up and was at a repair shop getting an official assessment," Josh said. "OK", Robert said, "I'd encourage you to call the insured back. Seek to acknowledge his frustrations. We appreciate that he's upset and recognize that a ball was dropped. We want to fully understand his situation so that we can best be in a position to constructively help. We won't leave him hanging. We won't leave him "fighting" with an insurance company. If we didn't do our job properly in the past for him, we'll do it right now and find a way to either reduce his loss exposure or eat it ourselves. You can tell him this now and ask for him to work with us in providing whatever additional information he can as he gets it. Can you run with this for us Josh?"

Josh took the direction and was happy to escape without the tongue lashing he anticipated. Josh had certainly approached the conversation with Robert from a defensive perspective. Understandably so, no one wants to present bad news, especially when their actions are likely the root cause of the bad news. Robert knew there was plenty to be learned from this experience and there was no value in attacks of any kind at this point. Seeking information to better understand the situation and extent of the problem was priority number one for them. From here they could determine how to reduce the financial impact of this issue on the insured. Finally, they would then determine how accountability internally would be allocated. What would A Priori need to do differently in order to prevent this type of circumstance from rearing its ugly head again down the road?

Robert wanted to give more thought to the issue Josh had just brought forth, but he knew that the main event of the day was a meeting with one of A Priori's longest standing vendors. It was an insurance market that A Priori had represented for decades. The meeting had been called a bit out of the blue and at the request of the market. Distracted with thoughts bouncing between the trucking customer's loss and this afternoon's looming market meeting, Robert felt the additional pull of his stomach grumbling.

No Such Thing as a Free Lunch

THE MARKET MEETING WAS to be early afternoon at 14:00. First, Robert had a lunch with Tom, his VP Finance. Tom, was a rarity within A Priori. That is, he had only been with the brokerage for just over a year. Tom was in his late 30s. He had come to A Priori after spending the first years of his career learning the hands on of bookkeeping, accounting, and finance with a manufacturing outfit. He had put himself through night school and achieved a CMA designation some years ago. He was qualified and competent in his role. His physical appearances reflected his capabilities. He was neither short nor tall. Neither was he fat nor skinny. And, finally, neither was he striking nor homely. He reflected a stereotypical non-descript. He was somewhat forgettable. His presence didn't exert itself forcefully. He was simply, there.

Robert and Tom opted to walk to a local deli which was part of a strip mall close to their office. The walk took only a few minutes and on this still freezing January day, took even less as it was more of a scared sprint. Stomping their feet to rid their shoes of the snow that stuck with them, they selected a table in a corner of the restaurant which offered a little bit of privacy.

Robert enjoyed his one on ones with his Management Team. He remained committed to having lunch with each of them at least once a month in order to gauge their perspective and sense of priorities.

Tom asked Robert if he wanted the usual and offered to get it while Robert relaxed and held their table. Robert thought this was a bit odd as it was he who typically both paid and ordered lunch, but acquiesced to Tom nonetheless by offering his thanks. Robert was able to enjoy a moment with his thoughts while Tom got in line to order their sandwiches. This deli hadn't been around quite as long as A Priori had, but it certainly had a business life longer than Robert's. Robert wondered about how many of the customers were regulars like he and others from A Priori. What kept people like us coming back? It wasn't the setting as it was nothing special. The floor was a stale gray colored commercial linoleum that presented itself less and less nowadays. The walls which weren't obscured by shelves stacked with spices for sale were covered by wallpaper. A tacky floral pattern littered the wall in a way that may be coming back into style. Robert just didn't pay attention to the home decorating trends that seemed to be the rage on TV and what was left of the few magazines on the shelves of grocery stores. Robert didn't think the proximity either would be a reason for coming back repeatedly over the years as there were plenty of other food options in this strip mall which he had never even considered going to. Sure, the food was good, but not renown. There were no newspaper clippings cluttering the wall presenting reviews or other publicity related to famous owners or patrons. This was just a humble family run business making decent food and looking after its customers.

Robert reflected on the idea that this business wasn't much different than his own. They both depended on helping people access what they need when they need it and they try to do it for the same people reliably day after day. Neither business depended on expensive outgoing advertising like radio ads or newspaper listings. It was satisfied customers spreading the word of their experience that fueled most new business for both this restaurant and A Priori Insurance. The lifetime value of each customer was something neither business likely spent enough time thinking about, but both businesses were dependent on repeat business for their extended existences. After all, he'd been coming here for close to twenty years averaging a visit a week or more at $30 a pop. His cerebral calculator chugged away at the math. Was he crazy or is it possible he had actually spent over $30,000 at this place? He went through it again. $30 x 50 week is $1,500 x 20 years is $30,000. Wow. And he wasn't done yet. That is, with having lunch at this place.

Too much time alone with the thoughts bouncing around one's brain can be informational Robert mused. Finally, Tom returned with their lunches. "Lunch is served", said Tom. "Here's your usual". The usual for Robert was what would seem to most as a mystery meat, but for Robert brought back smells, tastes, and memories from coming here with his father decades ago. The three types of smoked Pastrami covered in authentic Provone cheese still steaming from being toasted in the oven while wafting the sweet smell of home baked sourdough. No other nonsense needed to dilute the deliciousness. Nice try, Quiznos, he thought, but you've got nothing on this beauty. This sandwich would be washed down with a San Pelligrino sparkling water and its flavor would linger even after a few pieces of peppermint gum would be unleashed on undoing the spices.

"Thanks, Tom, appreciate you getting lunch today, can't wait to enjoy it." Robert took his first bite as did Tom and they bantered a bit about their past weekends. Tom was engaged and had nuptials looming in the Spring. Tom thanked Robert for making time for these lunches. He observed that it was useful to get the time together to discuss projects specific to his sphere of influence. Tom said, "I really enjoy working with A Priori and you, Bob. I've been with you now for just over a year. During that time, I feel like we've made some progress in Finance. We've tightened up our month end reporting from 10 days to 5 days. We've also created some better data digging with our current systems that has allowed us to create a more meaningful KPI (Key Performance Indicator) for Sue's Sales Staff. That's our PIF Count per customer." Tom paused talking and nodded while looking at Robert seeking acknowledgement, understanding, and, more importantly, approval.

Robert presented his poker face. Emotionless Eddie he called it. He sought to narrow his eyes a bit to reflect both intensity and interest without conveying agreement or acquiescence. He worked hard to be conscious about how he presented himself. Robert had taken a continuing education seminar some years ago related to Executive Presence or EP they called it. He had thought it malarkey at the time, but was warming up to it as he continued to read about it. Robert reflected back what he'd heard from Tom, "Yes, Tom, Sue definitely appreciates having the PIF data readily available as a tool to facilitate her Sales Management efforts. The month end reporting has been helpful as well. A Priori is glad to have you." Tom, leaned forward, now more motivated to press on to the meat and potatoes of his ask. "Robert, as you know I'm getting married in less than two months. Isabelle and I made a commitment on a new home this past weekend. I don't have to tell you that life's getting more expensive every year." Robert interjected, "Congratulations on your commitment, Tom, what are you after?" Tom, continued, "I've done some research, checked with some industry publications/job boards and talked with some of my peers from school, for a CMA, now a CPA with the joined designations, with over three years of work experience, I am being underpaid at A Priori. I'd like a 15% raise."

Boom, there it was, Robert knew he shouldn't be surprised by these kinds of requests after ten plus years leading a business with more than twenty employees. He now employed over forty staff, and these kinds of asks seemed to arise often. He also knew that he needed to do better on the HR front. He was a bit exposed in this area as A Priori had no formal Performance Management program. No one really did performance reviews regularly with staff. Sue did stay on top of our sales team, but even he didn't own responsibility reliably for managing annual reviews with his own Management Team. He had been meaning to address this gap and had it somewhere on his to do list. He also knew exactly where a road paved with good intentions leads. "Intention is Insolence, Execution is Everything" he recalled his father saying to him.

Bringing his thoughts back to Tom's ask, Robert was wondering a bit why he was not just taken aback but viscerally mad. It was too soon for the Pastrami to be protesting. He'd only had a couple of bites. Tom had been with A Priori for just over a year. He was the shortest serving member of A Priori's Team. His performance had been decent to date, but nothing special. Sure, his main "win" for the year had been tightening up month end reporting. However, the goal had been to move from 10 days to 3 days so achieving 5 was an improvement, but sub-par relative to expectations. We also had a few losses relative to budget on expense control. Things like IT and Professional Fees were two things that sprung to mind where expenses had exceeded budget by more than a little.

Moreover, he had been part of the budgeting process for the current year which was just under way. He knew full well that A Priori had budgeted 5% as COLA increases to Salaries & Wages. Robert had thought 5% for Cost of Living Allowance as reasonable and generous in an era of well under 2% inflation. How did Tom, a finance guy no less, make this ask at 300% what he knows we allocated? That seems distasteful. Robert was also reeling from how Tom had framed his ask. Sure, he had led with his "win", and couldn't really continue with other work related performances as there just hadn't been any, but imposing personal need as a reason for a pay increase was a pretty rookie approach. Robert has enough business concerns to worry about before he can get emotionally engaged in what houses, cars, TVs, and stuff his staff choose to purchase. If they're spending more than they make, that's not Robert's responsibility, is it?

Deep in his thoughts, Robert still worked hard to control his outer appearances. This was getting hard as Emotionless Eddie was morphing into Ornery Oscar. Robert recalled a separate quote he had written down somewhere from management guru, Peter Drucker, "Leaders owe it to the organization and their fellow workers not to tolerate non-performing people in important jobs." Though, Robert wasn't ready to consider Tom a non-performer just yet, he certainly didn't consider him beyond meeting expectations. Robert could see Tom wondering if he should continue making his case as Robert had been lost in thought long enough to create an awkward pause in the conversation. Robert heard another of his father's phrases ringing in his ears, "Don't demur, defer." Robert recognized there was no value to debating Tom's request with him in that moment and space. He needed to check his impulses and insert time for him to constructively prepare, then deliver a response to Tom.

"Tom, thanks for the feedback, let me digest this conversation for a little longer than we'll be digesting this delicious lunch. Let's look to meet a week from Wednesday to review this together." Tom wasn't prepared to push harder and was pleased that he had gotten his ask off his chest. He thanked Robert for listening and looked forward to more conversation on this subject next week. They enjoyed the balance of their lunch together bantering about the weather and with full, warm stomachs weren't as fast on their return dash to the office as they had been to get there.

Fond Thoughts
of Father

Back at his desk, Robert reflected on Tom's ask. Robert worked hard to not be entitled in his approach to work. Yes, he now owned a brokerage which had been his father's. Robert had negotiated the purchase from his father while he was still alive about five years ago. Robert had paid market price and had a nice fat bank debt in place to prove it. He hadn't been "given" anything. The last thing he wanted was to be thought of as a soft sybarite. He didn't see himself as entitled and only wanted the opportunity to earn his way. He wished for his staff to share the same sentiment he had.

Robert's father, George, had passed away almost two years ago now. He had suffered a catastrophic heart attack while showering one Monday morning before work. George was missed by many, but there wasn't a day that Robert didn't think about him and wish for one more day of some advice and insight from him.

All George had ever done was be in the brokerage business. He had started Pendleton Insurance in his early twenties and never looked back. He certainly endured some lean years along the way, but Pendleton Insurance had steadily sustained itself for well over a generation. Being a self-made small business man, these were the kind of people George connected with and was able to develop long lasting customer relationships with many of the trades and other small, construction related businesses that boomed in the 80s as the city exploded. This had been Pendleton's bread and butter. George didn't need PESTLE or SWOT analyses or multiple business degrees and designations to know that the relationship one had with one's customer is what mattered most.

Robert had learned Insurance at George's hip. There wasn't any aspect of what he knew that didn't flow from George. Most of the technical details Robert had learned while accompanying his father to customer visits at their various places of business. Business was generated more often than not by doing walkabouts at customer shops and warehouses. Pendleton Insurance had a meeting room. It was a misnomer to suggest it was a board room like the two sprawling ones A Priori now have, as Pendleton's meeting room had a two square foot table surrounded by two chairs. It was more like an interview cell at a jail house than a high-tech meeting room with multiple flat screen LCD TVs each emitting more wiring than an alien predator. The board table was some kind of funky designer special that had perfectly matching ergonomic chairs aligned in what seemed like a military formation around it.

This was just one example of how things had changed from Pendleton to A Priori. Now it was about preparing the office to welcome prospective customers instead of focusing on visiting them. Nowadays, it seemed more about making the office reflect professional prowess, poise, and profitability instead of focusing on what the customer's operations were about. Robert's reminiscing led him to acknowledge that some of these changes may not be for the better.

Robert missed many things about his departed dad, but most of all the time spent driving together from Pendleton's office to customers and back. This had been a big part of their time together back in the day. During these drives is where they sat and talked shop. George never had the radio on or listened to anything other than the thoughts in his mind. There was no better time to reflect on how to be useful and add value to customers than when driving. Most of Pendleton's customer base wasn't at the epicenter of downtown, but in surrounding growing areas that would be swallowed by the city over the years. The drives were on relaxed secondary highways and roads instead of stuck in sweltering, bumper to bumper traffic.

Robert's mind wandered to a story that had often resurfaced in conversations with his dad. It is one that George had sought to impart to all that worked with him as well. Robert's dad would talk about the Renaissance days hundreds of years ago in Western Europe and a role that developed in Italy known as an Anteambulo.

An Anteambulo was considered by many as a "slave" as a "detested" position one that was beneath anyone serious. The job was to act as an assistant or servant to wealthy businessmen, aristocrats, or noblemen. As an assistant, the Anteambulo's function was to set up appointments for their boss and ensure they got safely to those meetings. They would carry their boss' stuff and accompany them there. At its core, the function of an Anteambulo was to "clear the path". To free the friction such that the boss could get things done. The word itself was comprised of two parts: Ante and Ambulo. Ante means in front and Ambulo means to walk. Translated literally, the word Anteambulo was in front of to walk or to walk in front of someone. This was a pretty accurate description of the literal function of an Anteambulo. Their job was often to physically walk in front of their "boss" and help make way, clearing the path of people, obstacles, and whatever else may be in the way.

In Renaissance Italy, many Anteambulo were artists or those aspiring to be whether painters, musicians, sculptors, writers, actors, or other form of creative type. Their function as an Anteambulo afforded them a stipend which scarcely supported them yet allowed time to pursue their craft. Many artists gladly took on this role as they recognized that working with the well heeled exposed them to the parts of society where decisions were being made and the action occurred. They used their experiences as a muse for their creative work. For these artists, being an Anteambulo wasn't a bad thing. It offered both sustenance and fodder for their creative work. Unfortunately, some viewed this role as an insult or burden. They wallowed in anger fueling bitterness and resentment for their bosses and society at large. This attitude would preclude them from both adding value to their boss as well as completely closing off the opportunity of bettering themselves or their art. This, too, from George's perspective was comparable to how we treat our roles in the more modern world.

George supported his view of the value of interpreting any experience as having some kind of value with a quote from writer Jorge Luis Borges:

"A writer-and, I believe, generally all persons—must think that whatever happens to him or her is a resource. All things have been given to us for a purpose, and an artist must feel this more intensely. All that happens to us, including our humiliations, our misfortunes, our embarrassments, all is given to us as raw material, as clay, so that we may shape our art."

George liked the word Anteambulo and what the role represented. He thought it memorable and a wonderful metaphor to view our own role as supporters of our customers and staff. He considered his role as an Anteambulo to both client and staff. He viewed his function to "clear the path" for whomever he could. This perspective focused his attention on his customer's needs. He was constantly trying to ask questions about how their businesses work so he could understand what headaches they were encountering, where their difficulties and pain points were. Knowing these he could craft solutions that made their lives ever so slightly easier which was the route of what endeared George and Pendleton Insurance to so many.

George never had a CRM, he had a rolodex with the odd personal note scribbled on the card. George didn't have sales KPIs or Performance Management Programs. He was consumed with understanding what people needed, what was holding them back from their goals, and doing something in some small way to help them move forward. He implicitly knew that by helping enough people get what they want, he would be fairly and fully looked after.

When George did gather his sales staff to chat, the meetings never revolved around number of sales calls or quotas. These metrics simply didn't enter George's mind. George was fond of legendary investor, Warren Buffet. It wasn't just because of their mutual fondness for Dairy Queen Peanut Buster Parfaits, but because of Buffet's commonsense wisdom. George would brandish Buffetisms like a Gladiator unsheathing his sword, with flair he would offer a gem like "Beware of geeks bearing formulas."

He was consumed with helping his sales force help "clear the path" for their customers. Striving to be an Anteambulo offered the corollary benefit of keeping one humble and getting out of one's own head. It assuaged anxiety related to sales performance. It allowed one to not worry about what numbers or externally imposed metrics to achieve, but to be devoted to developing options for clients. "How can I help?" versus what can I get.

Some variation of "How did you clear the path today?" was continuously being asked by George to his sales force and leadership team. He reflected on this question many times a day related to his own activities. Robert knew of many occasions when George couldn't honestly answer concretely and positively in favor of a current or prospective customer this question, he would stay at the office and keep working until he had.

It was the core of George's operating system. It was both a focusing and filtering question. It focused one's attention on what's important and could be used against which to evaluate decisions.

Sadly, it seemed this sentiment was slipping at A Priori. Robert began to realize he had dropped the ball here. There would be no IT team if George was around. An idea that, perhaps, had been percolating, suddenly surfaced in Robert's mind. Maybe, his father's approach to business had been sound after all. Robert had a pang of regret for the times he had rolled his eyes at his father's "simplistic" approaches. He had considered the simple, steady, tried and true approach as simple minded and of evidence of being stuck in the past waiting to be passed by. Considering further, Robert conceived that simple didn't mean easy. Because an idea was clear didn't mean it was a given. The power of execution of getting things not just done, but done correctly involved discipline and coordination on many levels. This had become only too obvious in his few years in leadership.

Market Meeting

THE MEETING WAS SCHEDULED for 14:00 and Rundle Boardroom had been booked. Expected from Stalwart Insurance was A Priori's regional marketing rep. What was less expected was the presence of one of their Senior VPs.

The meeting itself wasn't part of the regular "calendar". A Priori typically had quarterly meetings with their markets. Markets were Insurance Companies whose products A Priori sold. The regular meetings would revolve around sales figures and issues about how the two businesses could work more seamlessly together. More often than not, these meetings were casual conversations of glad handling that were excuses to kill time until the fun part of heading out for a dinner, drinks, or round of golf in the summertime occurred.

Occasionally, a market was in a generous mood and was open to discussing some type of sales incentive. For example, if a market was aggressively trying to develop market share related to a specific geographic region or a specific type of insurance (coverage type) that they offered, the insurance company may offer an additional commission related to new business generated for a given period that fit their desired or targeted type. These, of course, were quite welcomed conversations.

Other nice to have conversations with markets revolved around CPC or Contingent Profit Commissions. These were, effectively, bonuses paid for past business provided. After all, it was not just the insurance sale that an insurance company was interested in, but insurance sales that resulted in the promise of insurance not being needed by purchasers of insurance. The quality of the business brought by a broker to an insurance company had a substantial influence on the overall profitability of the insurance company. If losses incurred by insureds were too high, then the cost of insurance generated may not be enough to cover losses obliged to payout, this was the dilemma with which an insurance company perpetually dances. They must seek to price their products competitively such that purchasers of insurance are willing to pay the premiums, yet they must also be strategic in terms of which risks (insureds) they are prepared to accept in order to avoid having to pay out large losses. Brokers did have influence in this area and ones that were viewed as being helpful to markets were rewarded with additional financial compensation. These CPC payments arose, largely, under "unknown" or "undefined" conditions from a broker's perspective. They could really only be determined once last year's policy had run its course and losses related to them were reasonably calculable.

Unfortunately, in recent years, A Priori hadn't been achieving CPCs on a predictable or regular basis. The only real adjustment that had been made was to remove these from A Priori's budgeting process and treating any CPCs received as a windfall as actual financial statements were prepared towards year end. This was always in the back of Robert's mind. He wanted to figure out a way to predictably earn these revenues. From his understanding, there was an industry standard or benchmark that better brokers were generating decent revenues reliably from CPCs. Perhaps, this could be something he proactively raises in this afternoon's discussion he thought to himself.

Attending with Robert would be A Priori's Sales Manager, Sue. She was a bit of a spitfire, a human dynamo. She was spirited and operated at a seemingly unsustainable level of energy. She had come to A Priori a number of years ago as a young mother who was a first class Tupperware salesperson. She had turned a hobby generating a few bucks into a significant income. Robert couldn't recall who had hired Sue, but it had worked out quite well for A Priori and, he hoped, for Sue.

Sue had no prior insurance industry background. This didn't hold her back from being an almost instant achiever with A Priori. Well within her first year as a Producer, she became A Priori's best salesperson. Her energy and remarkable ability to relate to others seemed to be her secrets to success. Sue's customer base had been broad. She dealt with friends within her community, former Tupperware clients, and any small business she came across. The clients were varied and voluminous, just like her frequently changing hairstyles.

Sue's personal sales prowess wasn't just quick to materialize, she was able to consistently maintain herself as a high-performer. After three years of being the best producer quarter after quarter for A Priori, George rewarded her by appointing her Sales Manager. She has been in this capacity for the past five years.

Unfortunately, as Sales Manager, Sue's dominant performance hadn't kept pace. She had struggled with trying to sustain a significant sales book herself. Trying to find the level that she could remain engaged with customers and developing her own business while being in a position to support and manage other sales staff productively was a delicate dilemma which balance had yet to be agreeably achieved. Additionally, Sue's sales successes had been more the product of her energy and effervescence and less the result of a focused plan or sales system. This remained the case today. Her absence of a consistent approach to carving out her own book of business led to difficulty with trying to communicate sales structure to other sales staff. Frustrations felt by sales staff as to A Priori's lack of structure and performance management had largely been brushed off as "excuses" or "quirks" of the "special" kind of people that populate the sales profession. This was a position that was getting harder to support as A Priori's turnover of sales staff seemed high. Often, it felt like A Priori had a revolving door through the sales department. It was tough to keep track of who was there. There were a few gray haired folk that were just used to the way things were and put their head down while doing their own thing, while the younger ones were more prone to turn-over. Robert knew that there was some work to be done in the Sales Department that would involve seeking to develop serious structure. Sue seemed to have some great ideas about how to improve things, but the answers typically seemed to lay "out there" with technology providers or training courses or consultants, but not within steps A Priori staff could concretely take daily.

Thinking about structure and sales, Robert turned his thoughts to Janet who would also be joining him in the impending conversation with Stalwart Insurance. Janet was serious minded and staid. She, too, had been a steady presence with A Priori for a significant period of time. Janet was outstanding at what she did. She had over twenty-five years of experience operating insurance brokerages most of her time being spent at A Priori. There wasn't an insurance problem she couldn't solve. Robert had absolute confidence in Janet's abilities. She was constantly seeking ideas on how to improve A Priori's operations.

Robert gathered Janet and Sue shortly before the scheduled meeting time. They sorted themselves into A Priori's Rundle Boardroom. When Robert received word that their guests had arrived to reception, he went to greet them. Visiting today from Stalwart Insurance were Darren, Stalwart's Senior VP, and Elaine, Stalwart's Marketing Representative for the region A Priori occupied.

When all were comfortably situated in the meeting room, Darren started, "I don't want to waste your guy's time, we've got some news that you probably don't want

to hear. As Churchill said, 'I will begin, therefore, by saying the most unpopular and most unwelcome thing.' As
you all know, Stalwart has had a few hiccups on the financial performance side of things. We're getting clobbered
in the Alberta marketplace. Due to government regulations, we just aren't able to raise our rates and it seems
like we're pushed into taking business that we don't really
want. We recognize the weight of these burdens are also
bourne by other companies participating in this market,
but Stalwart has been forced to make some decisions. As
a result, we're pulling back our distribution and limiting
access to our products to a handful of brokerages. Unfortunately, A Priori isn't on this list of remaining brokers."

Robert and his team sat in stunned silence. Being
brutally blindsided was bad enough. As a World War
II history buff, using Winston Churchill's words as a
cudgel was borderline sacrilege to Robert. He had had
a feeling of concern nagging at him about this meeting,
but had not conceived in any way that this disruptive of
an outcome would be the sole purpose of the conversation. Robert thought of offering a sarcastic response
like, I guess dinner's out, but just sat there stewing in his
juices, lost in thought. Darren saw that his audience was
taken aback and didn't have anything to say so he continued himself, "It has been several quarters in a row that A
Priori's loss ratio with Stalwart has exceeded 100%. This
puts its performance in the lower third of brokers Stalwart services. Unfortunately, Stalwart Insurance is like
any other business in that we can't afford to lose money
and expect to survive. We have to take action and dis-
continuing distribution through our lower performing

brokerages is the only option we've been able to agree upon internally."

Robert knew he had to say something. Part of him had enough internal optimism that, perhaps, he could come up with some genius insight on the spot that might change their minds. He glanced at both Sue and Janet then spoke, "I don't think we'd have been anymore surprised if the Tooth Fairy waltzed into this room, Darren, your news is more than a shock. We're aware that we've had a couple of rough quarters. We recognize that losses exceeding 100% of premiums are unsustainable. We don't see A Priori's performance much outside of industry averages. It is also an area of business we're working on improving. We recognize quality matters. Who we are selling to is as important as how much we're selling. We're always seeking to improve. Stalwart was our original market. They have been with us since my dad started our brokerage. They have been our longest standing relationship. Not to mention that A Priori has committed heavily over the years to support Stalwart and has grown its book with Stalwart over 300% in the past five years alone. Stalwart represents a major portion of our business. Is there any opportunity that you would reconsider your decision?"

Darren nodded sympathetically, acknowledging Robert's comments, "Bob, Stalwart Insurance appreciates our extensive relationship with each other. For what it's worth, this isn't a decision that came easily. We wrestled with this as a Management Group for quite some time. Unfortunately, the consensus was that we simply had to focus on quality. The market conditions are difficult. Our hands are being tied by regulatory rules and we have to find ways to restrict who we insure. Some risks just aren't worth it. The path forward for Stalwart is to reduce our distribution network and limit our products to brokers working with the cleanest clients."

Janet offered, "I echo Bob's surprise and disappointment. This is quite a shock. We have had some conversations ourselves in recent weeks related to market conditions. We had conceived of proactively proposing a reformation program whereby certain individual brokers had access limited as our analysis suggests we have a couple of poor performers who unduly do business with higher risk insureds. Much of A Priori losses on Stalwart business seem to stem from these couple of brokers. Would Stalwart be open to a conversation on this front?"

Darren responded without missing a beat, "I hear what you're saying, Janet, it is a topic we, too, discussed at length. We just don't have the luxury of being patient here. We are forced to take action now and the decision has been made. Unfortunately, all that's left to discuss is the details of transition. We want to be clear in that we aren't going to leave A Priori completely in the lurch. We will do what we can to help A Priori transition business from Stalwart."

Janet asked, "What kind of timeline are we talking here Darren? How quickly will Stalwart be cutting off new business for A Priori? We have producers in the field as we speak likely generating opportunities and quoting Stalwart coverage. For us to properly prepare a plan to mitigate damage from what you've just dropped at our feet, we'll need at least 90 days to transition existing activity. That's before we even begin to discuss rolling over renewal business elsewhere."

Darren firmly interjected, "Stalwart won't be accepting any new business from A Priori as of the end of this month." Talk about getting kicked when you're already down, Robert thought. Sensing that this "conversation" could get ugly quickly, Robert sought to dial things down by offering, "OK, Darren, I think we're grasping Stalwart's position with painful precision. Though we're not pleased with the decision, we understand it and will own what we need to do for A Priori from here. Can we wrap this up so that we can chew on this further together? We will commit to getting back to you with a proposed action plan to move forward by Friday. Can you work with us on this?

Dan seemed just as interested in ending the meeting as did A Priori's team. He had said what he needed to say and set the direction. There was no more need for continuing the conversation. On behalf of Stalwart, Dan conceded to Robert's request. The attendees mutually agreed to have a proposal to Stalwart by the end of the week that would set out the terms of winding down A Priori's book of Stalwart business. This largely implied transitioning existing business as it renewed and A Priori would need to find a new home for these clients. The parties bid each other good day, thanked each other for their respective times, and agreed to be in touch. The air had long ago left Rundle Boardroom and once Stalwart's delegates departed, A Priori's team sat in ashen silence.

Robert offered, "I don't know about you two," looking at Sue and Janet, "but this news was completely unexpected. That caught me off guard. I did not conceive of the seriousness or jeopardy we clearly had with this market relationship. I propose we take 15 minutes, review our calendars and seek to set aside at least another hour together right here, right now to brainstorm next steps. Can you two make time to accommodate?" Both Sue and Janet agreed, acknowledging the urgency of the circumstance. They each left to ensure their calendar was freed up and communicate to their reports that they would be continuing a meeting. They all understood implicitly that the conversation just had would have ripple down ramifications through A Priori and their local insurance marketplace. They each knew to not reveal anything about the meeting just completed to anyone they chatted with in the short time they were apart.

Returned to the Rundle room, the mood had not improved. There were three glum faces staring awkwardly at each other. It remained a stunned silence separating them while each pondered the impact this change would have on their respective areas of influence. Robert invited each to offer their thoughts. Sue jumped in and her feelings were evident. "That was crap. I can't believe Stalwart can even do this. It seems completely unfair. We have almost 20% of our customer base with policies involving Stalwart. Some of our brokers are almost exclusively representing Stalwart. We have clients that have never bought anything other than a Stalwart policy from us. We will definitely be losing customers and even some brokers. I can think of a couple right off the bat that are heavily dependent on Stalwart. If they can't access this market, they don't have anything to sell. They'll be seeking the market with another brokerage before sticking around here. Forget budget for this year. We're toast.

There's no way we're hitting our growth targets. I'm scared we're likely to lose ground now." Sue sat disappointed and dejected.

Robert couldn't help but nod in agreement. "I hear you, Sue, I appreciate your anger. Right now I feel like this is absolutely an attack on A Priori. You're spot on in observing the potential pain we will undoubtedly feel on several fronts. Our largest market, poof, gone. Too many of our "good" brokers selling exclusively through this channel. They will be hit where it hurts, right in the pocketbook, and quickly. I still can't wrap my head around the fact that the reason this brokerage ever became a business was because of developing a relationship with Stalwart Insurance. They have been our first, longest, and largest market relationship forever." Robert paused and in that moment realized that Stalwart was not only A Priori's longest market relationship, but the last remaining one that had been in place since his father's time. George had many, deep personal relationships that had lasted decades with staff from Stalwart. Robert felt a sense of shame tingling down his spine. He felt like he, personally, was failing his father. He didn't like the feeling at all.

Robert turned to Janet and asked, "Janet, Sue's offered a candid perspective. What are your initial thoughts?" Janet was more measured in her response. It wasn't infused with intense anger as much as Sue. Janet reflected more resignation. She seemed to already have moved to accepting the reality of the news and be thinking through impacts. "Stalwart's news is a surprise, a shock even. I, too, feel hurt by it. I didn't hear any room in the conversation for negotiation. This seems like a fait accompli. It's done in their minds and a senior person like Dan delivering the message makes it crystal clear, in my mind, where we stand. We simply don't have the luxury of wallowing in self-pity. We need to pick ourselves up, dust ourselves off, and get on with things. We've had transitions between markets before. This is good news. No question this will be the biggest one we've done in terms of the number of policies and premium dollars affected. We've got two key decisions to make and no time to waste."

Janet continued, "I understood Stalwart's position to be that we need to stop sending new business opportunities to them by the end of the month. This gives us three weeks to develop and implement a plan to offer an alternative to Stalwart for new, incoming business opportunities." Robert and Sue agreed with Janet's assessment and both appreciated her helping them transition from negative thoughts to proactively managing the problem they were collectively facing.

"Second, we need to manage all existing Stalwart business as it renews. We need to communicate well in advance (ideally, 60 days) to impacted insureds letting them know that their existing insurer is no longer available to them through A Priori, we then need to develop a process for our sales staff to pursue to offer suitable options. The better we do in these areas, the better our chances at stemming the flow of lost business that will be coming."

Again, Robert and Sue passively assented to Janet's insight, grateful for her calm contribution. Janet observed,

"Time pressure is our biggest challenge. We need to plan to contact each of our other existing markets, especially our remaining top four. Our focus should be to seek to interest one or more of these to willingly absorb a portion of business moving from Stalwart. Some of our markets may be aware of Stalwart's issues and be seeking to step into this business aggressively. There may even be the opportunity for a commission override of some sort of new business incentive. We should be seeking something here to help offset some of the business that we'll sadly see squandered." Janet paused further pondering what she had just spoken about.

Sue took the opportunity to offer, "Janet's right, there may be a silver lining in this cloud after all. We have heard rumblings on the street that Intrepid Insurance is seeking to further insert themselves in our marketplace. We have definitely seen them price themselves positively. That is, more favorably for insureds in recent months. Our concern has been their internal ability to manage an influx of business. We consider them a smaller player out of our available markets and there just may not be sufficient resources to handle an inrush of business that we're talking about here. We've been reluctant to send much business opportunity their way as a result. Nonetheless, this would be a great market to have an exploratory conversation with sooner than later."

Robert interjected, "Great suggestion Sue. Perhaps, our first step is to package details about our existing Stalwart book and present it to our other core markets plus a few other smaller ones with whom we dabble? If we were to do this, what information should we include, and how quickly can we get on it?" Janet didn't miss a beat, "We would need to generate some reports. Specifically, a list of active policies sorted by Expiry Date. This will tell us both the volume and distribution of business. We'll then need to condense this information into a digestible table for prospective markets to consider. We want them to know the amount of business and a decent idea of how it distributes throughout the calendar year. We'll also want to provide accurate information as to coverage types – what kind of business is it? Clarity here will help us determine which of A Priori's markets may be best suited to consider absorbing some or all of this business. We'll also need to present this information coupled with data specific to A Priori's support of each market we're considering presenting Stalwart opportunity to. That is, we and they will want to know how much of this business, if any, are we already sending to market X? Do they have an appetite for more? How much more? This is just a start giving this only a minute of thought. We'll come up with additional things to include once we dive into this. We should be able to get started on this as early as tomorrow and put a dent in it by late Wednesday. Our initial limitation may be getting Stalwart to cough up some data as we'll have limitations in our current systems."

Talking with Sue and Janet was helping Robert settle down his frazzled nerves. The day had been difficult, but the afternoon had taken a swift turn for the worse. Robert came to appreciate the diverse skill set of Sue and Janet even more as the conversation continued. Robert recalled conversations he'd had with Patrick Hasburgh, a neighbor of his for a short period. Patrick had been the man behind creating Hollywood hits like 21 Jump Street and The A Team. Sure, Hollywood had its A-Team, but A Priori had its own. Robert was hoping he wouldn't be considered the B.A. Baracus of the group as he felt his attitude had been less than constructive as the news originally arrived. He was grateful he had acquitted himself somewhat civilly as only a few years ago his temper would have likely gotten the better of him and he would have either lashed out in hostility or with overt sarcasm. Neither would have been helpful in any way and Robert was relieved he was able to demonstrate self-control better today than in the past.

"Thanks, Janet, these are sound suggestions. Can I count on you to take the lead on this front and attack this first thing tomorrow morning?" Before, giving Janet a chance to respond, Robert continued, "Once you have even a working summary of relevant information, let's seek to meet tomorrow afternoon with hopes of determining to which markets we will offer this opportunity." Janet nodded concurrently scribbling notes while Robert kept on, "Sue, not sure where your thoughts are with respect to keeping this news under wraps from your sales team? I'm thinking we want to keep a lid on this until we have some clarity as to direction we're taking. There's no point disheartening the team without offering a light at the end of the tunnel. Unfortunately, we just don't have that right now. What do you think about waiting until next Monday, at the earliest, to have a full-on Sales Meeting on this topic?"

Sue was on the same page as Robert. Silence was strength. No point in pulling fire alarms when the exits were all locked down. Nothing good would come of that. "Sounds good to me Bob. We've got a lot of work to do. My biggest fear is Stalwart's insistence on cutting off in the near term. We've only got a few weeks until the end of the month. If I understood Dan correctly, he's saying we need to find a home for new business and renewals by then. I'm confident we can have options available to manage new business opportunity distribution by then, I'm terrified about the idea of managing renewals in that short of a period. Frankly, I think this would put us off-side regulatory requirements." Janet jumped in, "You're right Sue, the Insurance Regulations require that we communicate to our insureds a minimum of 60 days prior to their current coverage expiry any change in Insurance Company for whatever reason. This should be something we clarify with Dan and ensure that Stalwart is supportive of managing any renewals for at least sixty days. Ideally, for at least sixty days post month end. It would be a more logical time for a cut off as it would be the end of Q1. This would reduce one major headache for us and manage regulatory risk. Bob, can you contact Dan tomorrow to seek clarity on this point for us?"

Robert agreed. They all had a bit more color in their cheeks now from the constructive conversation. Robert suggested they wind down the meeting, go back to their respective offices, and go on with their days for the short balance of the afternoon. They agreed to keep this amongst themselves until they were able to meet again tomorrow and formalize a game plan.

Frank's Text

Wow, what a day this had become, Robert thought to himself as he sat in his office. He definitely felt the urge to decompress, to blow off some stress. In his younger days, he would have gone to the gym and thrown around some heavy weights. His joints weren't what they used to be and he hadn't seen the inside of a gym since Carly Rae Jepsen was carving up the pop charts. It had been a few years. He at least had an evening of no responsibility to look forward to. His kids were both at separate friends' houses and would be dropped off at home. His wife was committed to curling with some friends. He just wanted to get home and spend some time with his ukulele. Robert had picked up a ukulele a few months back with the hope of being able to practice with his daughter who played the instrument for school. More importantly, he wanted to learn a song or two to play for her later this Spring at her birthday party. He was too old to become a meterosexual, manbun sporting, hipster, but was enjoying the mental focus he got while engrossed in learning something again.

Robert was trying to teach himself a song from the band Rise Against. He was trying to learn track three which featured the acoustics of a ukulele. However, he often lost focus and lingered on listening to the rest of the album as his learning stalled. The distraction was worth it as the album was fantastic. Reflecting on the rotten day he'd just plodded through, he mulled some lyrics,

"Keeping up appearances, don't break now, or buckle from the weight.

Take time to laugh, but don't laugh too loud.

Do you feel the pressure building, the anger spilling out now...

Meanwhile the cracks are formed on the masks we've worn up til now.

We are far from perfect..."

Robert looked down to check a text that had come in on his cellphone. He saw it was from his friend, Frank. The text read, "Buddy, it's been a while. What are you up to? Have time for some pops? Want to meet at Brennigans after work?" Robert didn't need long to think about responding. Frank was a buddy from University who also was in the insurance business. They had gotten their start around the same time. Frank ran an outfit that was substantially bigger than A Priori. Tanenbaum's Insurance had been around for over thirty years. Robert hated the name, he thought it sounded like talking while eating an apple. Frank began working there after graduating from University about eighteen years ago. Eugene Tanenbaum had been the founder and Frank began at the bottom of the organization. He, actually, started in the mailroom. His job was to receive and sort incoming mail. In those days, the volumes of mail were substantial and this could occupy the majority of a young person's day. He moved into accounting and up from there. Frank negotiated a buyout of Eugene's business five years ago. The business has probably doubled in the last five years. Through the acquisition, Frank made no effort to either rename or rebrand the organization. He stuck with tradition. Robert couldn't criticize him, Frank had to be doing something right based on the types of cars parked outside his office. Things were going well. Robert typed a text, "Sure, would be great to see you. I have a pass for the evening. See you at Brennie's for 17:30."

Robert called his get togethers with his friend, "Frank Conversations". It wasn't just because his name was Frank, but because Frank lived his namesake. He was as honest and open as they come. You got exactly the same guy every time. He was consistent and honest in thought, word, and action. There was no false pretense put forth by Frank. He was the antithesis of Facebook Frank. He never put on airs or presented only the best parts of himself or his business. He was humble and comfortable enough to talk about his problems. He was fine with talking about his progress as well, but rarely led with it. It's true that he has an objective track record that speaks for itself, but he was satisfied in his own skin and wasn't overtly seeking status or recognition amongst his peers. Frank was something Robert could never quite put his finger on. Frank was a different guy, in a great way. For as long as Robert had known Frank, over twenty years, Frank had been a consistent friend. Robert looked forward to spending some time with his friend this evening and forgot about the ukulele.

Driving To
Meet Frank

ROBERT LEFT THE OFFICE at quarter past five. Most staff worked from 08:30 to 17:00 with an hour lunch. A few folk straddled the "standard" work day as some liked to manage their work earlier with less people around to avoid distractions and traffic. While others liked to burn the midnight oil so to speak.

The weather hadn't improved. It was still frightfully cold with continued snow falling. Another almost 10 cm of fresh stuff had piled up during the day. Robert was grateful he hadn't left with the clock punchers a few minutes earlier as traffic would be snarled up for twice as long as normal. Though the 15 minute head start others had wouldn't help them get home any quicker, Robert looked forward to heading towards downtown, against the flow of dense traffic of the masses leaving the core. He anticipated a lighter load of vehicles on his side of the median.

Pulling out of A Priori's parking lot, Robert's phone connected automatically with the vehicle stereo and another Rise Against song played softly through the speakers.

"When the weight we carry breaks us, we're tempted to stay down.

But every road to recovery starts at the breakdown."

Robert wasn't worried about a breakdown, but he was tired. He was slowly succumbing to ongoing overwhelm which led to increasingly negative thoughts about his many business issues. Work used to be a lot more fun when he wasn't in charge. Bearing the burden of responsibility across all issues takes its toll. He wondered how many of his staff, especially his Management Team, would be going home tonight consumed with thoughts about even just one of the multiple issues that had surfaced today.

Robert rolled into Brennigans shortly before 17:30. He had been right about traffic. Even more so on a cold, snowy day, people weren't heading downtown but doing anything they could to get home and stay off the roads for the night. Robert looked forward to parking not just his car but his thoughts about business problems for even a few hours while visiting with Frank. He left his phone in the car and swiftly stepped from the Sportswagon shuffling snow in multiple directions as he made his way inside.

Brennigans

ROBERT'S EYES ADJUSTED QUICKLY to the dark interior of the bar as it was already dark outside. He saw Frank comfortably situated in a plush booth across the bar gesturing to him. He reflexively smiled and moved towards Frank. "Good to see you Frank, cold enough out there for you," Robert greeted Frank. "You don't have to tell me how cold it was, I walked in this morning, great to see you buddy," Frank responded. Robert wondered whether Frank was losing his marbles once and for all. He did have a proclivity for pedalling a bike to work in the summer time, part of some kind of competition he did with staff, but walking in today's weather, that seemed somewhat suicidal. Robert couldn't resist, he chortled, "you're nuts what's wrong in your life that you needed to walk to work today, are you acting out your inner Earnest Shackleton?" Frank laughed good naturedly, "No, I couldn't get the Beemer going this morning. Battery has given up once and for all. Dealer was kind enough to arrange to pick it up midday and manage some repairs on it. Instead of waiting for the courtesy car, I just started plodding to work, I even passed a snowplow that had been stuck." Robert nodded acknowledging Frank's recount while sipping on the water waiting for him. Frank continued, "It was definitely cold but I like to think I was more relaxed when I got to the office than most of the others that fumbled in later all frazzled and out of sorts." Robert nodded further in full agreement as he recognized that the state in which he arrived this morning had likely shaped his view of all events that subsequently transpired.

The waitress arrived to check in on them and they took a moment to order a round of beers. After ordering, Robert observed, "I saw your rig in the parking lot outside, the dealership obviously got after taking care of it for you." "Yes", Frank replied, "the dealership has been excellent. They were able to send someone over and get it boosted, drove it to their shop, diagnosed issues, and replace battery and alternator within a few hours. They even dropped it by the office late this afternoon so that I could drive it here." Robert made a mental note as that was a level of service his dealership had never reached. Not even close. He was lucky to get a fresh cup of coffee while waiting interminably for a simple oil change. How could one European luxury car dealership be so different than another?

Moving on from cars, Frank asked Robert, "How's business over at A Priori, you still growing gangbusters?" Robert thought for a minute. It's true, our topline revenue remained not just resilient but forward moving. A Priori sales continued to increase year over year. However, the profit level wasn't keeping pace. The margin was slowly shrinking and this was a nagging pain point for Robert. "Yes, we're still growing, but I honestly don't know how or why sometimes," Robert replied. "A wiseman once told me a quote from a prominent environmentalist, Edward Abbey," Frank said. "Oh, what's that", asked Robert? Frank noted, "Growth for the sake of growth is the ideology of a cancer cell."

Robert chewed on what Frank had just offered. It resonated within Robert. "Wow", he said, "that sure sounds a lot like us these days, we're constantly talking about growth and patting ourselves on the back as to any kind of increase in revenues, but there's simply no rhyme or reason to how we're going about it. Meanwhile, our profits remain stagnant. They aren't keeping pace with our revenue growth. It sure seems like something may be sick. Who was the wise person that told you that quote?"

Smiling, Frank said, "Your dad, George told me that one quite a few years ago when I was starting out. I didn't think too much about it at the time, but it really has become a cautionary principle we are constantly discussing. We use it to keep our minds consumed with bottom line performance."

"Another gem along the same vein he used to say often was 'It's not what you make, it's what you keep.'" Robert nodded and smiled a bit. He had heard that line a number of times. Frank observed, "Too many of us in our personal lives are consumed with what we're making, what's our salary, what bonus am I entitled to, and things like that. We're not thinking about what the tax implications are or how we should structure our affairs to reduce tax burdens. It's the same for our businesses. We seem to think growth of the top line is an indication of power or prowess. What's our market share? Who cares if we can barely sustain ourselves. The bottom line is what matters both in business and in life. Your father was conscious about that constantly."

They enjoyed a few sips of beer and some casual conversation for a few minutes until Robert noted, "Frank, I really was looking forward to spending some time with you this evening. Having a bummer of a day, I wanted to get together, hang out, have some beers, and shoot the breeze about anything but work related stuff. But, I just can't help myself. I've watched you move forward slowly but surely over the years without getting stressed out. Meanwhile, you've built yourself a great business. What's your secret? How have you done it?"

Insights from Frank

"BOB, I'M HAPPY TO relay what we've done at our shop in recent years. I'd hate, though, to call it advice. Another quote I came across some time ago read along the lines of 'all advice is autobiographical, I see your life through the lens of my life.' I heard that to suggest that people's advice is based on their own experiences. They don't know and can't know about your experience the way you can and, therefore, can't see the differences. It's up to the receiver to scrutinize and critically evaluate any incoming 'advice'."

Robert couldn't argue with Frank's insight. Frank Frank was in fine form this evening. He wasn't interested in talking about how amazing he was or what success they were having. He only wanted to offer information from the perspective of will it help. This was something Robert sorely needed.

Frank sat for a moment. Took a long pull on his pint, then said "I don't eat like I used to, this evening being an exception. I can't go out to the clubs all night, then pound back a plate of Chinese food at 2am. I can't eat dessert with every meal. To be healthy, we need to be more conscious of what we put into ourselves. We need to consume food with a purpose. We need to select quality over quantity. Well, choosing what business to take on and with whom is very much the same idea. Taking on any and all business because it's there at our doorstep seems fun for a while, just like heading back for seconds at the breakfast buffet. But a few hours later you're paying for it as your pants are stretched and your mind is slow and groggy. Accepting customers casually is similar in that your bloated business is slow and groggy to respond. It doesn't know in what specific way it is serving its customers as it can't even define who its customers are. Being a better businessman begins with becoming choosier. Choosier about what kinds of products and services you want to sell as well as being clear as to what kind of customers you want to serve."

Frank had offered a mouthful of wisdom packed into a few sentences. Robert thought of the food they had ordered and momentarily contemplated the coming calamari. I'm glad I chose that food he thought to himself yet softly said, "I get it, I should have looked at the salad menu", Robert said while patting his protruding paunch. They both took a moment to laugh at themselves.

"Did your dad ever tell you about the "6 Ps of Planning"?" Robert, smiled and nodded, "yes, he told that one to me a number of times. It's probably the one I hated the most and tried to tune out because it was almost reflexively paraded out in all kinds of odd circumstances."

"Prior Planning Prevents Piss Poor Performance", parroted Robert and Frank concurrently while laughing.

Robert said, "I heard that one when I didn't dress properly for the weather when out for a family walk, when asking for a sleepover last minute as a kid, and pretty much anytime I asked for anything. I haven't really thought much about this phrase in a long time, if ever. I had pretty much trained myself to tune it out without realizing how spot on it had been. Looking back now, I'm guessing it was my dad's effort to try to teach some personal responsibility? If I had taken even a few minutes to think about what I was about to do or where I was about to go or what I wanted to get later today, then I could prepare and plan to increase the chances of actually achieving what I wanted or better enjoying an experience."

"Yup", Frank responded, "It really is remarkable how applicable "The 6 Ps of Planning" are to so many circumstances in life. Your dad introduced the concept to me from the perspective of taking a few minutes to proactively plan one's day the evening before. Either using the last few minutes of one's work day to think through and prioritize their 'to-dos' for tomorrow or doing this at the end of the day at home before going to bed. He observed that too many of us go through life in pure reactive mode. We just show up and see what happens. We let the wind blow us in any direction without giving an ounce of thought to what is important for us to accomplish. He properly pointed out that anyone who has achieved in any arena has done so largely because of focused effort."

Their food arrived. Frank had ordered a pound of chicken wings split evenly between suicide and honey garlic. They could both feel the heat of the suicide spices emanating from the plate as the waitress dropped the food off. Both of their eyes began to water a little bit in anticipation. Robert had ordered some Calamari and salt and pepper riblets. All dishes were perfectly paired for their pallets and the beers they were enjoying. There wasn't anything green or looking remotely like a vegetable in sight. They thanked the waitress for their food and complimented each other for their culinary expertise. They were both quiet for a couple of minutes while they enjoyed their first few bites.

"Awareness and intention, basically both attributes of personal responsibility, were at the heart of all of George's insights. From The 6 Ps of Planning, to Give Yourself a Chance, to BIB", Frank said as he tucked his serviette into his shirt to use as a bib. "Bib? What does that one mean?" Robert asked while he frowned at Frank's regressive fashion. "BIB stands for Boring is Beautiful", Frank recounted, "Boring is Beautiful reflects that we benefit by reducing the number of choices available to us to reduce decision fatigue, for example. Going to work at the same time, the same way is an example of something we naturally do as a routine, and developing routines that help us accomplish what we want to do are vital to keeping us on track."

"BIB can also act as a reminder to avoid the flavor of the month of new ideas that are always in vogue offered in blogs, podcasts, and continuing education seminars. Instead of chasing new, unproven concepts, we use BIB as a guideline to keep us committed to basic, tried, and true concepts that we know have worked in the past just like my menu selection this evening."

It was a good thing that Frank was sporting his make-shift bib as while he talked he gestured with his hands while holding a chicken wing. The honey garlic ones had been heavily bathed in the sweet, juicy sauce. A long, lingering blob dripped from the held wing onto his bib. Frank noticed, swept it up with his other finger and licked it. "Ummm, umm, good. I love spoiling myself once in a while and eating this crap." Robert had to agree as he was very much enjoying his Calamari which was as fresh and succulent as he had hoped.

George as Mentor

"FRANK, I HAVE TO ask, how do you know so many of my dad's 'sayings'?" Frank responded to Robert's question, "It's a bit surprising to me that you ask, I had always figured you knew of George and my monthly meetings." Robert looked quizzically at Frank simultaneously shrugging his shoulders indicating unequivocally he had no knowledge of what Frank was speaking about. Frank continued, "your dad was my mentor, he took an active interest in helping me develop both myself professionally as well as my business. From the moment I got my license and summoned up the courage to ask him for some guidance, he stepped up and gave generously of his time month after month for years. I wouldn't have achieved any of the success we've had the good fortune to enjoy without him."

Frank paused to take a sip of his beer, then continued, "Remember the Seinfeld episode where George Costanza comes to the realization that every decision he seems to be making turns out to be the wrong one? Recognizing this, Costanza decides to do the opposite of whatever his instincts are. He frames this as an alter-ego, "Opposite George". Costanza's life takes several giant leaps forward. He experiences both career and relationship progress almost instantly. Well, Bob, your Dad, George, helped me become Opposite George in my own life. I was making a mess of things and pursuing directions that weren't being met with progress. I was making things more difficult than they needed. Your Dad, took the time to work with me and helped me realize 180 degree turnaround in the success of my decisions."

Robert's thoughts turned inward. He thought about a few years back when Frank and his dad likely began their conversations. It had been a difficult time for Robert. He hadn't embraced the Insurance Industry. He fell into it more as a default than as a decision. He had been wandering around almost aimlessly for years muddling here and fiddling there. Full of bright ideas and optimism but absent commitment and work ethic. He had been mired in misery in what he has since come to call his LAD phase.

Reading Robert's mind, Frank said, "remember your LAD phase, Bob?" Somewhat lost in his own thoughts, Robert nodded and mumbled acknowledgement. "You weren't the most fun to be around, were you? Your dad was deeply worried. He loved you very much and wanted desperately for you to develop. He was wise enough to know that pushing you or pointing out your gaps was only going to be met with resistance so he did what must have been incredibly painful for him, he let you be and gave you the freedom to fail." The frankness of Frank's words hit Robert hard and the knowledge cut deep.

Robert's LAD phase was a time in his life he'd rather forget. Robert had developed the acronym to reflect the negative attributes that had been the focus of his life for that period. LAD stood for Lazy, Alcoholic, and Dark. These three variables were a vicious cycle that afflicted Robert for a couple of years as a young adult.

Not having a clear path, he opted to avoid thinking about the future by drinking. When drinking, he stayed out late which compromised his ability to get started the next day. The apathy felt daily led to negative thinking and complaints. Thoughts were inwardly focused about what he was missing and why life was unfair. He became lost in a circling toilet bowl of being lazy, drowning pain or seeking distraction through drinking, followed by dark thoughts. He had since come to realize the dangerous path on which he'd been, though had never even conceived the pain he had caused others with his actions. Robert was grateful that he developed a sense of the downward trend he had been on and woke up to get serious. Spending time with Frank had been a key part of the transition. He was realizing Frank's past help ever more clearly through tonight's conversation. Robert's thoughts turned to regret as he wondered of this wasted period and squandered opportunity to spend time with and learn from his father. Time and lessons he could never get back.

Frank could see Robert was reeling from the insight while doing his best to digest it. He smiled at Robert and offered "I see you're hurting. You should know that your dad loved you throughout your time as a young LAD. As importantly, he had complete confidence that you'd get through it. Not so sure that I shared that confidence," he smiled. "He also got to see you get serious about yourself and your contributions to A Priori. You don't need to be stuck in the past worried about what might have been. You're doing just fine."

Frank went on to offer, "I think your favorite Band, Rise Against, sums things up well with their lyrics:

'In every color we shine, A tapestry of scars.

With every step we're growing stronger, we're moving onwards, we're finding right ways in spite the wrong ones. We're finding the beauty in what you've ignored. We are far from perfect, but perfect as we are...'

The past is the past, let's not dwell on it. You've made great progress. I am convinced you are making George proud with your stewardship of A Priori, even though, by the sounds of it, it may not feel like it today."

Robert was amazed of Frank's ability to insightfully include lyrics that meant so much to him.

"You've got to remember, Bob, being a broker was never a 'Plan B' for me. I didn't end up here as a result of closing off other doors. I knew I wanted to be part of the insurance business since early days in University. Frankly, I really knew I wanted to be a broker, not just involved in insurance. Being a broker has always mattered and continues to matter to me. I hope it does for you, too."

Sure, Robert enjoyed what he did and was grateful for the lifestyle that being a broker had afforded him over the years. As he had dabbled without enthusiasm as a younger lad at several other paths, the passion and direction Frank clearly had seemed foreign to him. Robert was compelled to understand Frank's position more.

He asked, "Frank, I do envy your clarity and sense of purpose. What is it about being a broker that you find so meaningful?" Leaning forward in the booth, Frank almost grew in stature, energized by the question.

"Bob, it is a privilege to sell insurance to the kinds of people Tanenbaum targets. We are all about supporting small business owners. These folks are the lifeblood of our economy. They independently, with their own initiative, start something from nothing in order to provide for their families. In order to take these risks, insurance is an expense they bear from day one. They can't get backing financially without having insurance in place. If they're successful on any level, they are now able to further contribute to our economy by purchasing things and hiring others. All of these imply additional insurance requirements. Without being able to access insurance, these entrepreneurs would be stifled from stepping up. Effectively, we're helping people protect their priorities. I admire the risks and self-reliance entrepreneurs take. Seeing ourselves as a key support partner to their process is a big part of what we try to keep front of mind at Tanenbaum Insurance.

"Protecting People's Priorities...I like it. That is what we're trying to do." Robert mused. "Without a doubt", Frank continued, "This idea is at the core of our Customer 4Cs. It's the driver behind Care. We are always asking ourselves and our customers about their priorities. What are they trying to accomplish? Where will they be in five years? It's not just about their physical possessions or business assets that we're looking to offer protection or coverage. We try to get to know as much as we can. We want customers for life. One corollary of this approach is that we are Choosy about our customers. We don't want to do business with everybody."

"Can you tell me about how you may apply some of these ideas to an area like your customers?" Robert asked. "Sure, we use the Customer 4Cs as a framework around which we build out our customer experience efforts. The 4Cs are <u>Choose</u> Customers, then preserve the <u>Control</u>, <u>Custody</u>, and <u>Care</u> of the Customer.

Choosing Customers

BETWEEN THE CALAMARI, BEERS, and coffee, it wasn't just Frank's insights that were being ingested. Robert was struggling to make sense of Frank's last comments. Choosing Customers? What is this all about? This seemed to run counter to every business instinct he had. A Priori didn't say No to doing business with anyone. They welcomed anyone. Any business was good business from A Priori's perspective. Robert had to ask, "The idea of choosing who one wants to do business with seems counterintuitive to me. How do you determine the types of folk and businesses you want to serve?"

Frank shrugged, "Like so many things, the idea is simple but not easy. We recognize that with respect to customers, as is the case with so many aspects of business, less is more. We don't want to cater to everyone. We want to serve specific slices of the market that we can focus our limited resources around serving well. For example, a phrase we use at Tanenbaum to help us hone in on the type of customers we're chasing is "Make me happy and find more people like me." Pausing for effect, Frank went on, "I don't say this with any arrogance that I'm something special. We use this phrase not as an expression of me but for any of us that work at Tanenbaum's. We're, hopefully, folk that work hard, play hard. We try to achieve. We have had some success which allows us to have accumulated a few things. We need to protect these things because they matter to us. We respect what insurance offers us in terms of security for the things we care about. We don't want to make claims. We want to be responsible. It doesn't mean we're perfect, but it offers a clear description of the kinds of people we want to associate with as clients."

Robert nodded indicating that he was still listening. "I think I understand what you're saying. By determining who you want to say yes to in terms of selling insurance, you've created greater clarity as to who you're willing to say no to."

Frank said, "Exactly. A big part of getting clarity as to the kinds of customers we are seeking to serve also involves our markets. As part of our quarterly market conversations, we are asking them about the types of risks they are most comfortable with. What is good business for them? How can we help support their efforts to either grow or improve business quality? What are the attributes of insureds that are important for them? What information can we help collect and provide from insureds to help our markets with their risk assessments and underwriting processes? These are formal questions we push with our markets regularly. We don't let them get away with offering generic platitudes in return. We're also reviewing their financial performance proactively and seeking a sense of where they may struggle with losses on either the investment or underwriting sides of their business. We want to be offering suggestions or solutions to help our markets improve their coverages."

Robert recalled his dad quoting Estee Lauder with something to the effect of "If you want a good vendor, be a good customer." He had never understood what the quote meant or what his father was trying to say when they were out shopping for perfume for Robert's mom around Mother's Day in years past. Now, it seemed to speak right to what Frank was talking about and what A Priori was experiencing. Market relationships at A Priori were treated with a culture of complaint. Problems surfacing in the business were more often than not attributable to something outside A Priori's control. That is, the market was the problem. A new underwriting process was more restrictive imposing difficulties to A Priori staff for generating new business. A market's technology platform wasn't working properly. Market X is offering additional commission compensation, why isn't our Market Y doing the same. The list of "transgressions" was lengthy and this seemed to be the preparation A Priori had in advance of its quarterly meetings. Putting himself in a shared market's shoes, Robert began to see that the same market leaving meetings with A Priori and Tanenbaum would have a very different takeaway.

"Wow, Frank, this is another shot to the solar plexus. Our approach could not be more different than how you're suggesting Tanenbaum Insurance approaches its market relationships. It is no wonder that A Priori seems to be in a constant state of managing book transitions from one market to another. We're spending so much time responding to what we see as the chaotic whims of markets or forces outside of our control without so much as considering what our role in this turmoil may be. We would do well to get over ourselves and our expectations of what our markets should be doing to make our lives easier and spend some time thinking about how we can help them."

Frank was on a bit of a roll and steamed forwards, "We recognize we are an insurance broker and our value is in providing services that are meaningful to purchasers of insurance. We want to reduce our vulnerability as a broker to having business removed by markets going directly. This, today, being especially the case. We see markets that used to distribute across a number of smaller brokers pulling back and seeking to distribute only through substantial broker networks. Heck, we've even seen markets purchase these broker networks almost instantaneously getting themselves a focused distribution channel into an existing customer base. This is pending disaster for brokers. Once we've Chosen the kinds of people and businesses we want to support at Tanenbaum, we do everything we can to "Control" our customer. This isn't controlling their decision or limiting their choices, but focusing on us as their service provider. We want to hold all parts of the customer relationship and pass as little as possible to the insurance company."

Frank took a moment to bite into one of the spicy suicide wings and then had to slurp some suds to soften the shock. "Phew, these have some kick to them. I hope they don't fight back too hard tomorrow", Frank exclaimed, before he continued to tear away further at the hot wings. Meanwhile Robert was chewing on Frank's framework of 4Cs for Customers. He asked, "Before you sweat more beer than you drink, can you give me an idea of the other two Customer Cs, Custody and Care?"

Frank went on, "You bet, Custody refers to ensuring that any customer we have has a specific broker/customer service team assigned to them. We have teams that specialize in the types of business we target. We try to "fit" our customers to a team that is best suited to support them based on both their personalities and needs. This includes standard segregation by insurance type like personal versus commercial, for example. But usually includes further segmentation by class of insurance being purchased, geographic region/neighborhood, and even social interests and likes. The more our brokers are like their customers, the more likely they are to get along and be able to understand and support the customer needs. This is a continuous process and no assignment is set in stone. We ask our customers for input here and make changes. It's not a perfect process and we use it more as a focal point to ensure that Custody is seen as not ownership of a customer, but responsibility for. This leads us to the final Customer C of Care."

"Care is probably the most obvious of the four. It encompasses all parts of customer service. From our perspective, the objective is to seek to formalize a reliably repeatable process that can be taught to our team. We seek to regularly review and improve our customer experiences with us. Care really is the most important of the

4Cs for Customers. We want this to be the ultimate arbiter of decision making. The C of Care ensures that we are focused on the customer first. How can we help? What are their needs? What concerns do they have? What is unique about their circumstances? We're not trying to sell a boilerplate product to everyone. Different people want and need to be treated differently. We want to not only recognize it, but respect it, and be in a position to offer the desired difference.

From Coors
to Coffee

"FRANK, I CAN'T TELL·you how much I'm enjoying our conversation. I really appreciate you reaching out with your text this afternoon. I was quick to embrace the opportunity to blow off some steam and these beers have been awesome. However, I'm now less interested in turning this session into a runaway and would prefer to continue on the train tracks we're on. Are you ok with sticking around a bit longer and hanging out? I'd need to convert to coffee." Frank responded jokingly, "Happy to stick around Bob. I'm enjoying the conversation too. Am I so boring that you need caffeine stimulation to continue?"

"Not at all", Robert jumped in almost defensively, "I really am grateful for you willingly sharing your experiences. I want to ensure my mind is less cloudy and can focus on what you're offering. I also am reinvigorated to try to immediately take action on some of this starting tomorrow morning at A Priori. I want to be able to wake up fresh. I like your Customer 4Cs. I grasp them conceptually. Can you give me an example or two of specific business decisions you're making that help Tanenbaum Insurance increase customer "Control"?"

"I'd offer billing as our biggest example, Bob, of how we try to implement our concept of Control. We do our best to avoid Direct Bill payment options from our markets. Our goal is to be 100% Agency Bill. We're not there today, but this area has been a prime driver of our business processes and profits in recent years. It is our single largest area of growth." Robert wasn't sure if he was missing something or if Frank was now messing with him. He wouldn't put Frank past playing a bit of a joke and spinning a sideshow that was full of fiction. Maybe frank Frank was morphing into funny Frank? Robert asked, "Are the few beer we've had too many for you Frank? What are you talking about? How can doing some Agency Bill be Tanenbaum's biggest area of growth?"

Maybe it was Frank's turn to get a bit defensive. He offered, "Seriously, no joking, running our book increasingly on Agency Bill has been a game changer for us. In the past, we, certainly our sales force, were happy to take the path of least resistance and pass customer details and payments to our markets directly. The Accounts Receivables responsibility became that of the market. Customer questions about payments were handled by the markets, and so on. It was easy for us. We could see, though, that this was making us less useful to both our markets and our customers. Many touch points that customers could have had with our brokers were now occurring directly between the insurance company and the insured. We were removing ourselves from being useful to either of them. Taking the easy way is rarely the sustainable way. We also did a little math and started to notice the revenues our markets were generating from their payment plans. Not only were they getting all they needed to know about our customers, they were also making significant revenues from charges associated with the payment plans. We wanted to protect ourselves as a provider to our customers and seek to generate some additional revenues. Converting to Agency Bill from Direct Bill with selected markets has helped us achieve both goals."

Frank paused while the waitress brought their coffees and cleared their plates. Somehow during the conversation so far Robert and Frank had fully devoured their meals and left the plates cleaner than the dishwasher could do. Both Robert and Frank were momentarily sad to see the coffee in place of another round of IPAs, but they got over it quickly.

While adding some cream and stirring his coffee, Frank continued, "From a revenue perspective, focusing on Agency Bill business allows us to generate about 40% more revenues on existing business while doubling its profitability. I know this sounds dramatic, but let's walk through it. Our sweet spot, our focus, at Tanenbaum is small business owners. A $5,000 policy is quite common. On a typical commercial policy we may earn a commission of 12% or $600. From this we're paying our producers, our admin team, office overhead, utilities, computers & communications, marketing, and all other expenses. If we're doing a great job, we may end up with a net profit of 25%."

Frank paused for a sip of coffee, while Robert mumbled, "25%, we don't have a net profit anywhere near that. That is a big number." Frank observed, "It's taken us years to reliably get there, but it is with operational discipline that we've achieved it. We made a commitment to running our business focused on this outcome and were prepared to go backwards before we made progress. It wasn't and isn't easy, but it remains our operational target. Anyways, back to our $5,000 insurance sale that has generated us $600 in commission revenues. If things are operating with excellence, we'll net $150 to the bottom line. Are you with me so far, Bob?" Bob nodded. Frank continued, "If Tanenbaum presents a payment option for our client, we can generate an additional $250 of revenue on the same sale. Our revenue, therefore, has gone from $600 to $850 or has increased by about 40%. But..., but..., the net profit on the finance side is substantially higher. We can comfortably net $150 on the finance side. This is, effectively, doubling the net profit on the same sale." Pausing, for effect, Frank studied Robert's incredulity, then offered, "Bob, Tanenbaum does achieve a bottom line well in excess of 25%. I'm not saying this to brag. I'm offering it with the spirit of our conversation this evening, intended only to offer insight into the opportunity available for A Priori to unlock profits existing in your business."

"Frank, no need for the disclaimer. I have always respected your willingness to offer a quiet, yet candid perspective. I consider one of your greatest strengths the ability to operate your business without seeking status or showboating your success. I am grateful for your openness. Particularly, this evening's conversation, Frank, has been eye opening. I am deeply impressed with your success. Also, a little intimidated. I'm also feeling some bitterness and sadness for squandered opportunity. I've been busy feeling good about myself and what I feel I've achieved over the years at A Priori and it turns out not only have I not been in the same league as you, I'm not even in the same game."

"Chin up, buttercup", Frank jumped in before Robert could bring down the mood any further. "That's just the winter blues talking, Bob. You're doing just fine at A Priori, the business continues successfully and honors your father's efforts while providing plenty of jobs. Your staff enjoy working for you and you are a big part of several community initiatives. There's nothing to feel bad about. You're a lucky guy. No matter who we are, there's always room for improvement. These are the conversations I deeply care about. I love for nothing more than exploring ways to improve how we operate. I hope that our talk this evening has rekindled a fire that is inside of you that you'll seek to stoke regularly. It's nothing more than a decision, Bob. A decision you make to deliberate on basic business principles. I also hope that you recognize from tonight's conversations that you already have the answers. The answers aren't 'out there'", Frank said, waving his hands. "Newfangled, fancy, schmancy, highly educated business consultants don't have any secrets. No software offers a magical miracle that will rain customers from the sky tripping over themselves seeking to pay you. You just need to reconnect with some of the things George did when starting your brokerage. You know deep down what those things are, I'm just sharing a few of the things that we've had success with. It doesn't mean these are going to be 100% your answers. You don't want to just be another copycat. You need to determine what is important for A Priori to focus on. No one else can answer this besides you and your team. It doesn't matter what I'm doing. It doesn't matter what the latest, whiz-bang, offering is that's making its way through industry communications. You can't abdicate answering this for A Priori and be truly successful."

The Steering Wheel

ROBERT FELT LIKE HE was sitting in a light shop after all the 'a-ha' moments he had experienced during this evening's conversation were illuminating so brightly. He was also spinning a bit from thought to thought as there was just too much information to absorb. Frank sensed this and offered, "Bob, it is getting late and we seem to be the only clowns left in this place. Our poor waitress and the rest of the staff are likely itching to get out of here." Robert agreed, it was getting later and he wanted to get home and let some of tonight's new knowledge percolate for a little longer than the stuff they had just been drinking had. Frank continued, "Bob, thanks for listening to me this evening. Hopefully, there's a kernel of useful information for you in there somewhere. It's important you recognize that we're just scratching the surface of these ideas. We bounced around from one big idea to another with barely any depth. We certainly don't know enough to be useful just yet. Rushing headlong in any of the directions discussed is dangerous with the limited exposure we've had tonight. Each of these subjects is like an iceberg on its own. Where we've just touched the small amount above, the real meat and potatoes lie underneath. If you're interested, I look forward to having a regular conversation with you to talk more about these and any other business ideas."

"Frank, I can't thank you enough for the time. It is always great to see you and catch up. I can't believe we haven't talked shop like this for as long as I can remember. You've definitely given me a lot to think about. Between your Customer 4Cs and reminding me of the 6Ps of planning, I've got enough to keep me busy for a while seeking to apply these frameworks to A Priori's immediate issues." Frank nodded, "Agreed. If I could be bold enough to offer a recommendation, I'd encourage you to spend a bit of time thinking through tonight's conversation, then settle on the one idea you'd like to try to put into practice at A Priori. Don't try to do too much. Just pick one concept and seek to apply it on one aspect of your business. You can then better evaluate its impact, good, bad, or otherwise and adapt. Doing more is just diluting your efforts and confusing yourself and your staff." As enthused as Robert was, he nodded and tacitly agreed to Frank's suggestion. Robert asked, "Do you have time to meet in a week to keep me accountable to tonight's conversation?" "Sure", Frank said, "I'd be happy to meet again in about a week. Why don't we set up an outdoor play date? It looks like winter will stick around for a while. Do you want to meet next Tuesday or Wednesday later afternoon and go for a snow shoe? It's a great outdoor activity that isn't too exerting. The trails west of the city offer an accessible, beautiful place that is quiet and allows you to be alone with your thoughts. I think you'll get a lot out of just being on these trails. Don't worry, there's no learning curve to snow shoeing. Even I can do it." Alright, Robert thought reluctantly nodding his head. It's not an activity he would have recommended and not one he's done, but if it means he'll get to pick Frank's brain some more, Robert was in.

Having a minute alone in his car while letting it warm up in the cold, quiet night, Robert's phone connected with the car's stereo and more Rise Against lyrics came through the speakers:

"Are you gonna wait here for a sign to let you know now, are you gonna sit there paralyzed from what you've seen?

Or are you finally going to grip the wheel, I think you know how. Is this more than you expected it to be?

Don't wait for a miracle to tumble from the sky, to part the seas around you, turn water into wine.

Don't wait for a miracle, the world is passing by. The walls that all surround you are only in your mind.

The stage is set, the curtains pulled. Ready or not, it's time, on with the show."

The Drive Home

DRIVING HOME, THE ROADS were completely empty. The snow fall had stopped. Most other people were hiding at home escaping the elements. This afforded Robert the luxury of entertaining his thoughts while driving quietly through the dark streets. What a day. A whirlwind of emotions from the lows of how he left the office to feeling much better about things right now after spending hours with Frank. The business issues that Robert and A Priori were facing hadn't changed or been solved in the time he had dinner, but somehow, in some way, Robert had a newfound confidence that these challenges could be constructively met. There was light at the end of the tunnel. Robert wanted very much to honor Frank's generous contributions to tonight's conversation. Robert didn't want to let the night end without having made at least a decision.

There had been a ton of great ideas offered by Frank this evening. Robert was convinced that Frank's final advice suggesting that just a single idea be explored initially was sound. He wanted to find something that he could use as a common driver across his current circumstances. While reviewing all of Frank's offerings, Robert liked more and more the Customer C of Care. In fact, the more he thought about it, the more it sounded exactly like his father's approach to being an Anteambulo. Clearing the Path and using the question "How can I help?" are at the essence of Care. This concept could be used as a guiding principle against which decisions are weighed.

A Priori could consider applying this idea in the impending market rollover with customers that would need to be moved from Stalwart Insurance. This undertaking will force brokers that have just been putting the same insurance coverage from the same insurance company in front of their customer year after year without even meeting with them to contact them and seek a meeting to discuss their insurance needs. Using Care as A Priori's North Star, it will be through conversations with A Priori customers that will help our staff determine who the best market will be. Robert also considered how packaging details about Stalwart customers will be helpful to present to insurance companies so that A Priori may proactively entice selected markets to grow business that is desirable for them. If we can help our markets see the potential of certain slices of our existing Stalwart business, we can have more options to present our impacted insureds.

Thinking about Tom and his ask, Robert conceived of an approach. He wanted to seriously explore expanding offering some kind of internal payment plan to customers for both the revenue opportunity Frank had mentioned as well as the ability to enhance and control the customer relationship better. Robert would task Tom with building out a business plan for this initiative and tie in an incentive to Tom's department that would eclipse what he had been asking for. If he's willing and able to come through, he'll jump at the opportunity and show Robert and A Priori that he's a go getter.

Finally, on the IT front, Robert realized that using Care and Clear the Path as decision drivers would work. The idea of how can we help or how can we clear the path being exclusively offered in respect to customers didn't have to be the case. It would be a philosophy A Priori would adopt and apply across all business departments.

Though Robert didn't have all the answers to each of his business challenges, he was increasingly confident that Care – Clearing the Path was going to be the primary driver of A Priori efforts come tomorrow.

A New Day

AFTER ROBERT'S SHORT BUT deep sleep, he bounded out of bed with an enthusiasm he hadn't felt in a long time. It was still dark and bitterly cold outside, but he had a renewed vigor. He wanted to get after it and start taking some formal actions post his conversation with Frank from the evening prior.

Even though daylight was still hours away, an idea dawned on Robert. For all the talk in industry circles and the business press about how "software was eating the world" that had consumed conventions, Robert now had an optimism for the future that had been pushed into the background. Many pundits had prognosticated on how Artificial Intelligence was disrupting entire industries and insurance wasn't exempt from these impending changes. Robert was coming to believe that A.I. indeed may be the future. Though, the A.I. he had in mind wasn't Artificial Intelligence, but it was Awareness and Intention. Two tried and true principles which he was convinced would become even more useful in times of change.

He was aware that he would be paving a path for A Priori. He dug up a quote he had written down in a notebook years ago from former Ford CEO, Alan Mullaly.

"Throughout my career and my life, there has been one essential truth: the biggest opportunity for improvement—in business, at home, and in life—is awareness."

Last night's conversation had awakened an awareness that had been asleep. In the dark of the new day, Robert was instilled with inspired intention.

About the Author

BEN SILLEM IS PRESIDENT of Broker Builder, a software and administrative services firm that specializes in supporting independent insurance brokerages in North America achieve financial success through development of In House Premium Finance services. An alumni of University of Calgary, Ben attended law school at the University of Alberta, has an MBA from the University of Leicester, and has achieved the Certified Marketing Executive (CME) designation. Ben enjoys living in and roaming the resort town of Invermere, BC with his wife and three sons. Learn more about how Broker Builder can help your brokerage unlock profits existing in your business by visiting www.brokerbuilder.ca.